5 SECONDS OF SUMMER

Test Your Super-Fan Status

Written by Stewart Allan

Edited by Bryony Jones
Design and cover design by Zoe Bradley

Picture Acknowledgements:
Front cover: David M. Benett / Getty Images

Picture section:
Page 1, AGF s.r.l. / Rex Features
Page 2, Frazer Harrison / Getty Images
Page 3, Stefania D'Alessandro / Getty Images
Page 4, D Dipasupil / Getty Images
Page 5, AGF s.r.l. / Rex Features
Page 6, AGF s.r.l. / Rex Features
Page 7, Stefania D'Alessandro / Getty Images
Page 8, Frazer Harrison / Getty Images

First edition for North America published in 2014 by Barron's Educational Series, Inc.

First published in Great Britain in 2014 by Buster Books, an imprint of Michael O'Mara Books Limited, 9 Lion Yard, Tremadoc Road, London SW4 7NQ

www.busterbooks.co.uk

Text copyright © Buster Books 2014

Artwork adapted from www.shutterstock.com

All inquiries should be addressed to:
Barron's Educational Series, Inc.
250 Wireless Boulevard
Hauppauge, NY 11788
www.barronseduc.com

PLEASE NOTE: This book is not affiliated with or endorsed by 5 Seconds of Summer or any of their publishers or licensees.

ISBN: 978-1-4380-0614-7

Date of Manufacture: August 2014
Manufactured by: B12V12G, Berryville, VA

Printed in the United States of America

9 8 7 6 5 4 3 2 1

5 SECONDS OF SUMMER

Test Your Super-Fan Status

BARRON'S

CONTENTS

ABOUT THIS BOOK

There's just no denying it, you are seriously obsessed with 5 Seconds Of Summer. You've seen all their videos, can sing along to every one of their amazing songs, and you and your BFFs are more than happy to spend hours discussing why each one of the boys is "just perfect."

Whether you've been a fan since the beginning and caught their earliest online videos or you first noticed the boys supporting 1D on their massive tours, you are now completely hooked on their super-catchy songs and are powerless to resist their charms. It's no wonder you can't get the words to "Kiss Me Kiss Me" out of your head!

So, how much do you really know about your four favorite boys? This book is packed with cool trivia, word puzzles, and quizzes to test your super-fan knowledge.

Are you ready for the challenge? Grab a pen and follow the instructions at the top of each page—you can check all your answers on **pages 90** to **95**. Don't stop until you get to the end and discover just how much of a 5SOS fan you really are.

PERFECT TEN

YOU THINK THE 5SOS BOYS ARE AS PERFECT AS CAN BE, AND YOU KNOW EVERYTHING THERE IS TO KNOW ABOUT THEM—RIGHT? TEST YOUR SUPER-FAN KNOWLEDGE AND SEE IF YOU CAN GET A PERFECT SCORE BY ANSWERING ALL TEN OF THESE QUESTIONS CORRECTLY. CHECK YOUR ANSWERS ON **PAGE 90**.

1. Which college were Luke, Michael, and Calum attending when they met?
   a. Southside View College
   b. East Valley College
   c. Norwest Christian College

2. Which member of 5SOS is the tallest?
   a. Luke
   b. Ashton
   c. Calum

3. 5SOS covered the song "Next To You" in one of their first YouTube videos. It was originally recorded by Chris Brown and featured which other singer?
   a. Justin Bieber
   b. Rihanna
   c. Pharrell Williams

4. Which famous clothing store is mentioned in the lyrics for the boys' song "She Looks So Perfect"?

   a. American Eagle

   b. Gap

   c. American Apparel

5. Which record company are the boys signed to?

   a. Sony

   b. Capitol

   c. Atlantic

6. Which member of the band came up with the name 5 Seconds Of Summer?

   a. Michael

   b. Luke

   c. Calum

7. In which London venue did 5SOS kick-off One Direction's 2012 *Take Me Home Tour*?

   a. Wembley Stadium

   b. The O2 Arena

   c. The Royal Albert Hall

8. All the boys in 5SOS are obsessed with Will Smith. Can you name the TV show that made him famous?

   a. *The Big Bang Theory*

   b. *Friends*

   c. *The Fresh Prince of Bel-Air*

9. What is the name of 5 Seconds Of Summer's own record label?

   a. Pants Down Records

   b. Hi Or Hey Records

   c. Perfect Records

10. Which of the two boys in the band share the same astrological sign?

   a. Luke and Ashton

   b. Michael and Luke

   c. Calum and Ashton

HE'S SO PERFECT: MICHAEL

DO YOU KNOW ALL THERE IS TO KNOW ABOUT 5 SECONDS OF SUMMER'S GUITAR-WIELDING WILD MAN? ANSWER THE QUESTIONS BELOW AND CHECK YOUR ANSWERS ON **PAGE 90** TO SEE IF YOU'RE MAD FOR MICHAEL.

1. What is Michael's middle name?

   a. Gordon

   b. Griffin

   c. Graham

2. Which character from the television show *Arrow* does Michael think he's in love with?

   a. Felicity

   b. Thea

   c. Laurel

3. Which is Michael's favorite chocolate bar?

   a. Hershey's

   b. Cadbury's Twirl

   c. Snickers

4. What is Michael's superhero name in the "Don't Stop" music video?

   a. Mike-Ro-Wave

   b. Mik-E-Mouse

   c. The Mighty Mike

5. What is Michael's favorite Disney movie?

   a. High School Musical

   b. Tangled

   c. Camp Rock

6. Which is Michael's favorite emoji?

   a. Eggplant

   b. Smiley face

   c. Broken heart

7. If Michael could learn another musical instrument, what would it be?

   a. Accordion

   b. Flute

   c. Trombone

8. What name does Michael think would be perfect for the band if they weren't called 5 Seconds Of Summer?

   a. Bromance

   b. Boomerang

   c. Pond Life

FOOD FOR THOUGHT

THE BOYS LOVE FOOD, BUT WHICH OF THEM SENT EACH OF THESE TASTY TWEETS? WRITE YOUR ANSWER UNDER EACH TWEET AND CHECK **PAGE 90**. ARE TOP MARKS ON THE MENU FOR YOU?

Just got a milkshake and a hotdog, feeling American

....

Just ordered a steak and chips two days in advance

....

Gonna make some French toast, cause I think I can do that, I'm not sure, I'll let ya know how it all pans out

....

I'm a frozen yoghurt addict

....

The boys are teasing me because I'm eating salad :(they're calling me salad boy

....

I tell you what, sausages around the world just aren't as good as Australian sausages...I'm very upset

....

THE STORY OF US

READ THE INCREDIBLE TRUE STORY OF HOW FOUR GUYS FROM AUSTRALIA BECAME ONE OF THE BIGGEST BANDS IN THE WORLD. FILL IN THE BLANKS TO GET THE WHOLE PICTURE AND PROVE YOU TRULY ARE A 5SOS SUPER-FAN. IF YOU NEED HELP YOU CAN FIND A LIST OF THE MISSING WORDS ON **PAGE 15**. CHECK YOUR ANSWERS ON **PAGE 90**.

Luke Hemmings, Michael Clifford, and Calum Hood met at

.... After hanging out and playing music together, they decided to start a band. It wasn't long

before, in early .... , the three guys began recording songs together.

They instantly knew they had something special and started posting videos of themselves singing other people's

songs on .... The boys were an instant hit, picking up hundreds of thousands of new fans each month.

As time passed, the boys knew they needed to find a

.... Soon they discovered Ashton Irwin, who became a full-time member of the band in the month

of .... 2011.

With the band now complete, the boys started writing their first songs together and soon they were ready to release their first EP. It was called .... and it gave 5SOS their first top-five hit on the Australian iTunes chart.

The boys were becoming an online phenomenon, posting more YouTube videos and gaining a massive following on Facebook and Twitter. Their international popularity really started to explode when One Direction's .... said he was a fan of the band and posted the boys' video for "Gotta Get Out" to his Twitter followers.

By the time they released the lead track from the *Somewhere New* EP as their Australian debut single, the 5SOS boys were unstoppable. Soon they were on the move and on a trip to London; they were writing with some brilliant songwriters, including Roy Stride from Scouting for Girls, James Bourne from Busted and Nick Hodgson from

....

Things took another unbelievable turn when One Direction asked the band to join them on their 2013 tour to support their album .... It was set to be a life-changing experience and one they would never forget. On February 23rd 2013, the boys kicked off the tour at the O2 Arena in ....

After nearly nine months on the road with One Direction across Britain, America and Australia, the boys returned home and decided it was time to get serious about their own music.

Soon they announced that they would be signing to .... Records and began planning the next stage of their world domination. It was going to be a long process, but the band began thinking about collecting enough songs to form their debut album.

In an interview with the *Fuse*, Calum explained, "We've written over .... songs now and we've finally whittled it down to 20 or 25," so it was obvious only the best of these was going to make the cut.

The first new song to see the light of day was "She Looks So Perfect." It became an instant smash, topping the charts in nearly 40 countries around the world. By the time their second single, "Don't Stop," was released in June 2014, they had made their American TV debut on the .... Awards show and were nominated for .... at the 2014 Kerrang! Awards.

As the boys geared up for the release of their album, tittled .... , they headed out on tour again with One Direction, starting their leg of the *Where We Are Tour* on May 23rd at Croke Park in .... , Ireland.

With all this going on it's amazing the band had a moment to do anything outside their tour schedule except eat and sleep, but on arriving back in the U.K. they found the time to record a new track with BBC Radio 1 DJ

.... called "Hearts Upon Our Sleeve" to

celebrate ....

With the album ready and another world tour under their belts, it looked like nothing could stop the four boys from becoming the biggest and best band in the world.

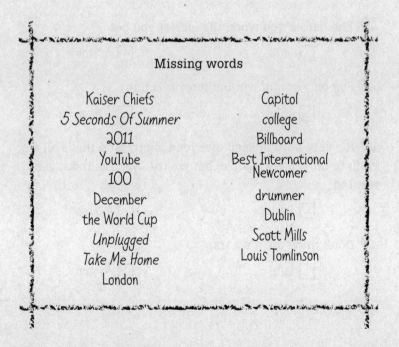

Missing words

Kaiser Chiefs	Capitol
5 Seconds Of Summer	college
2011	Billboard
YouTube	Best International Newcomer
100	
December	drummer
the World Cup	Dublin
Unplugged	Scott Mills
Take Me Home	Louis Tomlinson
London	

★ SO DEEP: LUKE VS ASHTON ★

THOSE 5SOS BOYS ARE DEEP THINKERS AND LOVE TO TWEET THEIR WORDS OF WISDOM TO FANS. CAN YOU TELL IF IT WAS LUKE OR ASHTON WHO SENT THE FOLLOWING TWEETS? PUT AN "X" IN THE CORRECT BOX AND CHECK THE ANSWERS ON **PAGE 91**.

The harder you work, the luckier you get

☐ Luke   ☐ Ashton

I've only got forever but forever is fine

☐ Luke   ☐ Ashton

It's very hard to keep everyone happy, and that's all we want to do, it's impossible, but we try. We take risks, you need to...

☐ Luke   ☐ Ashton

Don't grow up, it's a trap

☐ Luke   ☐ Ashton

Find something that makes you happy and don't let anyone take it away from you :-)

☐ Luke   ☐ Ashton

You won't find faith or hope down a telescope

☐ Luke   ☐ Ashton

You never find anything that you're looking for

☐ Luke   ☐ Ashton

You've got to be who you are, and not be scared...
Be strong.

☐ Luke   ☐ Ashton

This moment right now is one of the best times there will be in my life, I want to take a moment, to thank you, for giving us a chance

☐ Luke   ☐ Ashton

I wish happiness was untouchable, and nothing would hurt

☐ Luke   ☐ Ashton

HE'S SO PERFECT: LUKE

IS LUKE YOUR FAVORITE MEMBER OF 5 SECONDS OF SUMMER? DO YOU KNOW EVERYTHING THERE IS TO KNOW ABOUT 5SOS'S LEAD SINGER? CHECK **PAGE 91** TO SEE IF YOU'RE RIGHT.

1. What is Luke's middle name?
   a. Robert
   b. Randy
   c. Roger

2. Which Oscar winning Hollywood film actress does Luke have a massive crush on?
   a. Cate Blanchett
   b. Jennifer Lawrence
   c. Ann Hathaway

3. Which fruit does Luke think is underrated?
   a. Strawberries
   b. Watermelon
   c. Pineapple

4. What is Luke's superhero alter ego's name in the "Don't Stop" music video?

a. Luke Frystalker

b. Luke R. Round

c. Dr Fluke

5. Luke says he reminds himself of which character from the show *How I Met Your Mother*?

a. Ted

b. Barney

c. Marshall

6. What slogan is printed on Luke's T-shirt before he changes into his superhero costume at the beginning of the "Don't Stop" video?

a. You Complete Me

b. Keep Calm and Rock

c. Summer Love

7. What is Luke's favorite animal?

a. Kangaroo

b. Penguin

c. Lion

8. What is Luke's pet dog's name?

a. Patch

b. Molly

c. Kylie

CRACK THAT CROSSWORD

USE THE CLUES ON THE OPPOSITE PAGE TO HELP YOU FILL IN THE CROSSWORD BELOW. CHECK YOUR ANSWERS ON **PAGE 91**.

ACROSS

1. 5 Seconds Of Summer's first No.1 in the U.K. (3, 5, 2, 7)

6. Australian city where the boys went to school (6)

9. Name of the first 1D tour that 5SOS supported (4, 2, 4)

10. Chris Brown and Justin Bieber song that 5SOS covered (4, 2, 3)

11. "Teenage Dirtbag" was originally a hit for this band (7)

12. 5 Seconds Of Summer's own record label (2, 2, 3, 7)

DOWN

1. Surname of the original singer of "Give Me Love" (7)

2. Band who asked 5 Seconds Of Summer to join them on their *Where We Are Tour* in 2014 (3, 9)

3. 5SOS have written songs with the singer Alex Gaskarth. Name his band (3, 4, 3)

4. 5SOS's second U.K. single (4, 4)

5. Internet site where 5SOS first posted their videos (7)

7. Surname of the member of 1D who posted the video link to 5SOS's version of "Gotta Get Out" on his Twitter feed (9)

8. Ashton's middle name (8)

WHO SAID IT?

IF YOU'RE A TRUE SUPER-FAN YOU HANG ON EVERY WORD THAT LUKE, ASHTON, MICHAEL, AND CALUM HAVE TO SAY. SEE IF YOU CAN FIGURE OUT WHICH ONE OF THE BOYS SAID THE FOLLOWING QUOTES IN INTERVIEWS. ANSWERS ARE ON **PAGE 91**.

1. "We wanted to stay under the radar for as long as we could—now is the time for us to really show the world what we're about."

Who said it? ....

2. "We're not from a very nice area. None of us came from a lot of money."

Who said it? ....

3. "We totally sucked. But it just felt right between the four of us on stage."

Who said it? ....

4. "Our first show with 1D was pretty special ... we had to take it from garage playing to arena playing."

Who said it? ....

5. "It was just amazing. I just look up to him so much and when we were writing with him, just seeing him there and shaking his hand and him being like, 'It's nice to write with you', I was just so happy to be there."

Who said it? ....

6. "My favorite band, musically and live, is Paramore—I think they're incredible."

Who said it? ....

7. "I wanted a name that people could add their own name to like '5 Seconds Of Calum' but that's the only thing I was thinking about ... the other boys hated it."

Who said it? ....

8. "When the guys first started talking about it, we thought they were joking ... And now I look at my calendar in my iPhone and it goes from 'doing our thing, doing our thing, four shows at the O2 arena in two days!' It's crazy."

Who said it? ....

9. "We are the same guys as when we started - we just kinda look older now."

Who said it? ....

♪ TWEET TIME ♫

THE 5SOS BOYS LOVE TO TWEET. CAN YOU TELL WHICH ONE OF THEM SENT THESE TWEETS? FILL IN YOUR ANSWER AT THE BOTTOM OF THE PAGE AND CHECK **PAGE 92** TO SEE IF YOU ARE CORRECT.

🐦 Have you guys ever seen a wet koala... It is the scariest thing ever. Like ever

....

🐦 Fastest way to dry ya hair... Put on some heavy metal and head bang for 5 minutes

....

🐦 Thank god for this beanie, my hair is like krusty the clown today

....

🐦 There is a guy at the gym I go to, who just sits on the bike, not pedalling, and simply watches the Simpsons... Every day

....

🐦 Submarines are so underrated. Let's all take a moment to appreciate submarines

The mystery Tweeter is ....

1D BUDDIES

5SOS GOT THEIR BIG BREAK TOURING WITH ONE DIRECTION ON THEIR *TAKE ME HOME TOUR*. BUT DO YOU KNOW JUST HOW CONNECTED THE BANDS ARE? CHECK YOUR ANSWERS ON **PAGE 92**.

1. Which member of One Direction first tweeted that he'd been a fan of 5SOS "for a while" in November 2012?

....

2. What was 1D's second world tour with 5SOS called?

....

3. Calum and Michael star in a YouTube video lip-syncing to a "chipmunk" version of which 1D song?

....

4. In which American town and state did the first concert of the *Take Me Home Tour* take place?

....

5. Which member of 5SOS Tweeted the following to 1D: "Best song ever video is incredibleeee.. well done boys"?

....

 FANS FOR EVERYTHING

THE BOYS FROM 5 SECONDS OF SUMMER KNOW THAT WITHOUT THEIR FANS, THEY WOULDN'T BE WHERE THEY ARE NOW. READ THE QUOTES BELOW ABOUT THE JOURNEY THEY'VE MADE AND THEIR THOUGHTS ABOUT THEIR FANTASTIC FANBASE. CAN YOU FIGURE OUT WHO SAID EACH QUOTE? FIND THE ANSWERS ON **PAGE 92**.

1. "I'm a big fan of character, something individual in a person is amazing."

Who said it? ....

2. "I'd definitely date a fan. It would be like dating someone who likes your music, so it would be a bonus."

Who said it? ....

3. "We have fans all over the place now ... it's going to be great to try and visit EVERYWHERE too."

Who said it? ....

4. "Some of these countries we didn't even know existed. It's crazy. We could never dream of this in a million years."

Who said it? ....

5. "We said the other night ... We played a show in New York and we're from Sydney. It's not even in the same hemisphere."

Who said it? ....

6. "Ashton once got a Rubik's Cube thrown at him. It was like they were asking him to solve it or something."

Who said it? ....

7. "We are single and ready to mingle and eat Pringles."

Who said it? ....

8. "I think we've all got really good at dodging stuff on stage."

Who said it? ....

I LOVE 5SOS

SECRET GIG

CONGRATULATIONS, YOU'VE WON A COMPETITION TO BE A VIP GUEST AT A SECRET 5SOS GIG. UNFORTUNATELY, THE BOYS HAVE FORGOTTEN TO TELL YOU WHERE AND WHEN THE CONCERT IS TAKING PLACE. CAN YOU FIGURE OUT THE DETAILS FROM THE CLUES BELOW? THE ANSWERS ARE ON **PAGE 92.**

1. The gig will take place in the same city and venue as the 2014 Billboard Awards, where 5 Seconds Of Summer performed "She Looks So Perfect."

Where is it? ....

2. Can you figure out the date and time of the concert from the clues below:

   ⓐ. Date—the same as track five on the 5 Seconds Of Summer album

   ⓑ. Month—the same as the month Calum was born

   ⓒ. Time—the same as the date of Ashton's birthday in July

The gig is on .... (month) .... (date) at .... (time) pm.

3. The superstar guest who is rumored to be joining 5 Seconds Of Summer onstage for a very special performance is hidden in the wordsearch below. Can you find it? (Hint: their two names are separate.)

A	W	E	Q	P	K
H	K	V	U	E	H
W	B	A	N	R	G
G	J	X	T	R	Z
I	L	A	F	Y	L
T	N	M	Y	O	P

4. Hurrah! You've made it to the venue. If you can find where you are supposed to sit inside the concert hall, you will find a very special backstage pass hidden under the seat.

a. Entrance door number–the same as the number of tracks on the standard *5 Seconds Of Summer* album

b. Row letter–the same as the first letter of Ashton's middle name

c. Seat number–the same as Michael's birthdate

Use entrance number .... You are sitting in row

.... , seat number ....

5. Now all you have to do is figure out the secret combination to get you through the VIP door and into the backstage area. Answer the questions below and you will have the special six-digit code.

    a. What are the last two digits in the year Ashton was born?

    b. How many members of 5 Seconds Of Summer attended Norwest Christian College?

    c. What was the highest chart position for the *She Looks So Perfect* EP on the American Billboard Top 200?

    d. What date in July is Luke's birthday?

The secret combination is ....

Well done, you're in! What's the first thing you do when you see the boys?

....

....

....

TWEET TIME

THE 5SOS BOYS MIGHT JUST BE ADDICTED TO TWITTER. THEY LOVE TO KEEP YOU UP TO SPEED WITH EVERYTHING THEY DO AND EVERYWHERE THEY GO. CAN YOU FIGURE OUT WHO SENT THE TWEETS BELOW? CHECK YOUR ANSWER ON **PAGE 92.**

I'm wearing a black sock and a gray sock today and I feel awkward about it

....

Recording a sad song, gotta get my sad face on haha

....

I say cool beans way too much

....

You know you're tired when you fall asleep in the shower

....

I play guitar but she's into plumbers

....

quiffs aren't punk rock but neither am I so hey

....

I hate umbrellas

The mystery Tweeter is ....

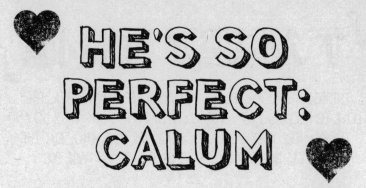

HE'S SO PERFECT: CALUM

DO YOU KNOW CALUM AS WELL AS YOU THINK? ANSWER THE FOLLOWING QUESTIONS ABOUT 5SOS'S CRAZY BASS GUITARIST AND CHECK HOW WELL YOU DID ON **PAGE 93**.

1. What is Calum's middle name?
- **a.** Tony
- **b.** Terence
- **c.** Thomas

2. Which famous American landmark does Calum plan to steal one day?
- **a.** The Grand Canyon
- **b.** The Statue of Liberty
- **c.** The White House

3. What is Calum's favorite ice cream flavor?
- **a.** Vanilla
- **b.** Mint chocolate
- **c.** Strawberry

4. Which U..S comedy is Calum's all time favorite television show?

   a. *Friends*

   b. *The Big Bang Theory*

   c. *30 Rock*

5. What is Calum's superhero name in the "Don't Stop" music video?

   a. Cal O' Ree

   b. Cal Pal

   c. Cal-Q-Lator

6. What does Calum think would be a great name for a jazz cover band?

   a. Sax Pistols

   b. Let's Talk About Sax

   c. Sax Bomb

7. Which celebrity would Calum most like to be stuck in an elevator with?

   a. Lady GaGa

   b. Usher

   c. Katy Perry

8. What is Calum's favorite pizza topping?

   a. Ham and pineapple

   b. Pepperoni

   c. Roasted vegetables

A PERFECT 5SOS DATE

YOU'RE PLANNING A VERY SPECIAL DATE WITH ONE OF THE 5SOS BOYS. THE ONLY PROBLEM IS YOU DON'T KNOW WHICH ONE YOU LIKE THE MOST. TAKE THE QUIZ BELOW, THEN FIND OUT YOUR PERFECT MATCH ON **PAGE 37**.

1. How would you like to work up an appetite for dinner?

   a. Snowboarding

   b. Soccer

   c. Ice skating

   d. Walking on the beach

2. What is your favorite hobby?

   a. Photography

   b. Science

   c. Computer games

   d. Animals

3. How would you describe yourself?

   a. Serious

   b. A good listener

   c. Sassy

   d. A nerd

4. What is your worst habit?

   a. You borrow other people's clothes without asking

   b. You skip dentist visits because you're scared

   c. You bite your nails

   d. You lose things all the time

5. What do you think is your best quality?

   a. You give the best hugs

   b. You don't judge people on how they look

   c. You don't let haters get you down

   d. You love sharing and giving to charity

6. You decide to set the mood by playing some music. Which of these albums do you choose?

   a. Blink 182–*Take Off Your Pants and Jacket*

   b. Queen–*Greatest Hits*

   c. Nickelback–*All the Right Reasons*

   d. Green Day–*Bullet In A Bible*

7. What are you going to cook your special guest?

   a. Pepperoni pizza

   b. Spaghetti

   c. Cheeseburgers

   d. Ham and pineapple pizza

8. You've got dinner all planned. What's on the menu
   for dessert?
   a. Pancakes
   b. Cookies-and-cream ice cream
   c. Chocolate chip ice cream
   d. Watermelon

9. It's time to pick something to watch after dinner.
   Which one of these movies do you choose?
   a. Monsters Inc.
   b. Anchorman
   c. Hercules
   d. Forrest Gump

10. You've still got time for an episode or two of your
    favorite TV show. Which do you choose?
    a. How I Met Your Mother
    b. Family Guy
    c. Friends
    d. Arrow

So you've planned the perfect date down to the smallest
details—now you just need to find out who would be the
best person to join you. Use the table on the next page to
score your answers, add them up and your grand total will
help you find out which one of the 5 Seconds Of Summer
boys is your perfect date.

1. a)1 b)2 c)3 d)4
2. a)3 b)1 c)4 d)2
3. a)1 b)3 c)4 d)2
4. a)2 b)4 c)3 d)1
5. a)1 b)4 c)2 d)3

6. a)1 b)4 c)2 d)3
7. a)1 b)3 c)4 d)2
8. a)2 b)1 c)3 d)4
9. a)1 b)2 c)3 d)4
10. a)1 b)3 c)2 d)4

If you scored 16 or under, Luke is your perfect 5SOS date.
Luke likes to blow off steam and have fun, but he's not afraid
to show his more serious side, too. He is quick to let you know
how he feels. Both romantics, you are a perfect combination.

If you scored 17 to 24, Calum is your perfect 5SOS date.
Calum is a team player. Like him, you know that good friends
are priceless and you like to be one of the gang. He speaks his
mind and is in touch with his inner nerd. With Calum in your
corner, there's no way you'll end up as a heartbreak girl.

If you scored 25 to 33, Ashton is your perfect 5SOS date.
Ashton might have a real crazy streak but he's also a great
listener. His artistic side means he knows lots about style, so
he would be perfect to take shopping. With Ashton, you might
just end up saying, "Kiss me, kiss me."

If you scored 34 to 40, Michael is your perfect 5SOS date.
There would never be a dull moment with you and Michael.
You both live life to the fullest. But Michael also knows when
it's time to get serious. He's the wild man of the band, but it
looks like you might just be the one to tame him, so don't stop
trying.

PERFECT DAY

HAVE YOU EVER WONDERED WHICH OF THE 5SOS BOYS WOULD BE YOUR PERFECT COMPANION FOR A FUN DAY OUT? ONE WHERE YOU SET THE RULES AND MAKE ALL THE DECISIONS? FOLLOW THE PATH TO FIND OUT WHICH OF THE 5SOS BOYS WOULD BE THE BEST TO SHARE YOUR PERFECT DAY.

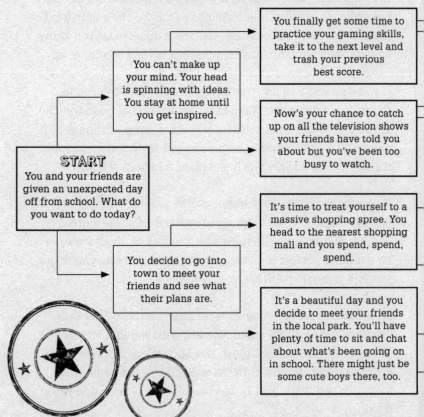

You finally get some time to practice your gaming skills, take it to the next level and trash your previous best score.

You can't make up your mind. Your head is spinning with ideas. You stay at home until you get inspired.

Now's your chance to catch up on all the television shows your friends have told you about but you've been too busy to watch.

START
You and your friends are given an unexpected day off from school. What do you want to do today?

It's time to treat yourself to a massive shopping spree. You head to the nearest shopping mall and you spend, spend, spend.

You decide to go into town to meet your friends and see what their plans are.

It's a beautiful day and you decide to meet your friends in the local park. You'll have plenty of time to sit and chat about what's been going on in school. There might just be some cute boys there, too.

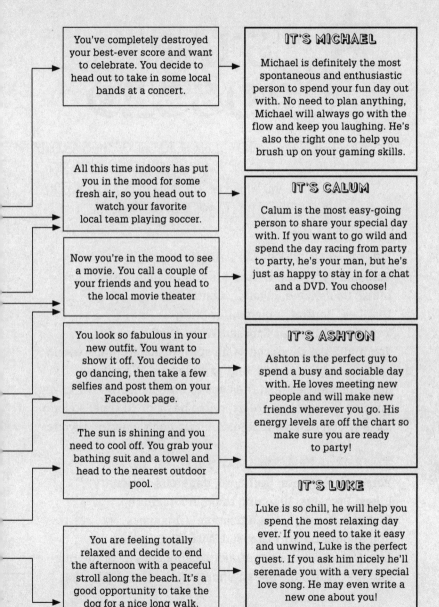

You've completely destroyed your best-ever score and want to celebrate. You decide to head out to take in some local bands at a concert.

IT'S MICHAEL

Michael is definitely the most spontaneous and enthusiastic person to spend your fun day out with. No need to plan anything, Michael will always go with the flow and keep you laughing. He's also the right one to help you brush up on your gaming skills.

All this time indoors has put you in the mood for some fresh air, so you head out to watch your favorite local team playing soccer.

IT'S CALUM

Calum is the most easy-going person to share your special day with. If you want to go wild and spend the day racing from party to party, he's your man, but he's just as happy to stay in for a chat and a DVD. You choose!

Now you're in the mood to see a movie. You call a couple of your friends and you head to the local movie theater

You look so fabulous in your new outfit. You want to show it off. You decide to go dancing, then take a few selfies and post them on your Facebook page.

IT'S ASHTON

Ashton is the perfect guy to spend a busy and sociable day with. He loves meeting new people and will make new friends wherever you go. His energy levels are off the chart so make sure you are ready to party!

The sun is shining and you need to cool off. You grab your bathing suit and a towel and head to the nearest outdoor pool.

IT'S LUKE

Luke is so chill, he will help you spend the most relaxing day ever. If you need to take it easy and unwind, Luke is the perfect guest. If you ask him nicely he'll serenade you with a very special love song. He may even write a new one about you!

You are feeling totally relaxed and decide to end the afternoon with a peaceful stroll along the beach. It's a good opportunity to take the dog for a nice long walk.

STAR CROSSED

IT'S YOUR FATE TO MEET AND GET CLOSE TO ONE OF THE 5 SECONDS OF SUMMER BOYS. FIND OUT WHAT YOUR ASTROLOGICAL SIGN SAYS ABOUT YOU AND WHICH OF THE BOYS IS IN YOUR DESTINY. DON'T FIGHT IT ... IT'S WRITTEN IN THE STARS.

ARIES (MARCH 21—APRIL 19)

Personality Traits: Creative, strong-willed, ambitious
Likes: Socializing, loyalty, spontaneity
Dislikes: Routine, injustice, waiting
You Should Be Star Crossed With: Luke
You and Luke share the same spirit of adventure, soaking up new sights, sounds, and experiences. It's always "the more the merrier" as far as you're both concerned, and your mission is to make sure everyone has a good time, so long as they don't show up late. You two don't wait for anyone.

TAURUS (APRIL 20—MAY 20)

Personality Traits: Stubborn, generous, visionary
Likes: Presents, listening to others, planning
Dislikes: Greed, disorganization, selfishness
You Should Be Star Crossed With: Calum
Like Calum, you're not afraid to think outside of the box and that can make life an unpredictable, wild ride. You

might put your foot down every now and then, but you're open to advice from others because you never know how your ideas are going to turn out.

GEMINI (MAY 21— JUNE 20)

Personality Traits: Unpredictable, imaginative, affectionate
Likes: Talking, new experiences, winning
Dislikes: Monotony, delays, indifference
You Should Be Star Crossed With: Ashton
Like Ashton, you are never quite sure which side of your personality is going to come out to play from one day to the next. Sometimes you are outrageous and loud and other times you are quiet and restrained. No matter what mood you are in, you always make sure there's plenty to talk about and keep everyone around you on their toes.

CANCER (JUNE 21— JULY 22)

Personality Traits: Traditional, compassionate, emotional
Likes: Time on your own, family, simplicity
Dislikes: Complications, interference, uncertainty
You Should Be Star Crossed With: Ashton
Like Ashton, you wear your heart on your sleeve and like the comfort of home as much as hitting the party scene. Ashton was the last to join the crazy world of 5SOS and he knows what it's like to want some downtime now and then.

LEO (JULY 23— AUGUST 22)

Personality Traits: Born leader, opinionated, brave
Likes: Challenges, being in charge, arguing
Dislikes: Taking orders, holding back, cowardice

You Should Be Star Crossed With: Michael

Like Michael, you like to take control of every situation and make sure everyone knows you're in charge. You are more than willing to listen to reason but you will defend your right to make decisions and never shy away from an argument. Just make sure everyone knows you like to win … it could turn into a long and bumpy night.

VIRGO (AUGUST 23—SEPTEMBER 22)

Personality Traits: Persuasive, intuitive, impatient
Likes: Analyzing, teamwork, entertaining
Dislikes: Selfishness, laziness, interference
You Should Be Star Crossed With: Calum

You share Calum's ability to keep the crowd entertained. You always seem to know exactly the right thing to say or do in any given situation and if someone gives you a problem to fix, as long as everyone lets you get on with it, you will sort it.

LIBRA (SEPTEMBER 23—OCTOBER 22)

Personality Traits: Impartial, perceptive, shy
Likes: Stability, nature, going to extremes
Dislikes: Arguments, dishonesty, clutter
You Should Be Star Crossed With: Luke

Like Luke, you can be a little shy in some situations, but are just as likely to be the center of attention if the mood strikes you. You like to have a routine and you share a very special talent with Luke—you can always see both sides of an argument. It definitely comes in handy with four opinionated boys in the band.

SCORPIO (OCTOBER 23— NOVEMBER 21)

Personality Traits: Determined, secretive, confident
Likes: Solving problems, privacy, focus
Dislikes: Being disorganized, liars, wavering
You Should Be Star Crossed With: Michael

You share your star sign with 5SOS's wild guitarist and you certainly have plenty in common. Like Michael, you are popular and out-going, and you are always looking for fun. Where you are is where the party is and you are determined to let everyone know that your way is the right way. Luckily you both have enough charm to make sure you get what you want.

SAGITTARIUS (NOVEMBER 22— DECEMBER 21)

Personality Traits: Intense, impatient, rational
Likes: Discovering new things, independence, quick results
Dislikes: Commitment, taking orders, being controlled
You Should Be Star Crossed With: Michael

Both you and Michael like your freedom. You want to stay in control of your own lives and never want to feel tied down. Michael would be perfect company on your own voyage of discovery, always ready to party, sharing your thirst for knowledge and new experiences ... just don't expect him to stay with you for ever.

CAPRICORN (DECEMBER 22— JANUARY 19)

Personality Traits: Intelligent, organized, trustworthy
Likes: Following a plan, free speech, listening
Dislikes: Criticism, chaos, gossip
You Should Be Star Crossed With: Luke

Luke shares your ability to be a caring friend when the need arises. You both think about things calmly and come up with the most sensible solution. You like to hear everyone else's opinion, but steer clear of gossip and hearsay. Luke often keeps the peace in the band. Like him, you will always advise your friends to talk things through rather than run away from a problem.

AQUARIUS (JANUARY 20— FEBRUARY 18)
Personality Traits: Unconventional, easy going, motivated
Likes: Loyalty, socializing, relaxing
Dislikes: Dishonesty, conflict, laziness
You Should Be Star Crossed With: Calum
Like the 5SOS bassist, you're quirky and want to make a mark with your style and ways of thinking. You both love to stay in touch with all your friends and don't worry if you have to keep on the move to see everyone. There's never a dull moment when you two are in the mood to party.

PISCES (FEBRUARY 19— MARCH 20)
Personality Traits: Thoughtful, trusting, determined
Likes: Time to think, generosity, family
Dislikes: Liars, pushiness, instability
You Should Be Star Crossed With: Ashton
Like Ashton, you can be too trusting and often fall for practical jokes. Fortunately, you both have a good sense of humor and will gladly laugh at yourselves. You like to stay close to your family and friends and enjoy nothing more than a night in, catching up and taking the time to unwind.

SONG SCRAMBLE

AS A TRUE SUPER-FAN YOU WILL HAVE SEEN ALL OF 5 SECONDS OF SUMMER'S YOUTUBE VIDEOS AND OWN ALL THEIR SINGLES AND EPS. YOU MUST KNOW ALL THE SONGS THEY'VE PERFORMED BACKWARD—BUT CAN YOU UNSCRAMBLE THE FOLLOWING SONG TITLES? CHECK YOUR ANSWERS ON **PAGE 93.**

1. "HES SOLOK OS RECPEFT"

....

2. "KREEBTHRAA RIGL"

....

3. "XENT OT OYU"

....

4. "NODT POST"

....

5. '"UTO FO YM MILIT"

....

6. "GLENSIH VELO FFRIAA"

....

7. "DOOG RLSIG"

....

8. "EEBSDI UYO"

....

Which is your favorite 5SOS song?

....

WHO WE ARE

STORMING THE CHARTS AROUND THE WORLD IN SUCH A SHORT SPACE OF TIME MEANS THE BOYS ARE VERY EAGER TO LET ALL THEIR NEW FANS KNOW EXACTLY WHAT KIND OF BAND THEY ARE. SEE IF YOU KNOW WHICH ONE OF THE BOYS SAID THE FOLLOWING QUOTES. CHECK OUT THE ANSWERS ON **PAGE 93**.

1. "We're not a boy band—we're a band."

Who said it? ....

2. "We have definitely been influenced by punk and rock bands, but we're not ashamed to say that we want to get our music to as many people as possible."

Who said it? ....

3. "People were already calling us the new One Direction in Australia, but in our minds we're a lot different from them. We play guitars. We're rockier. But we thought that if you put us right next to each other, it would actually show people how different we are."

Who said it? ....

4. "We don't want to be called the next One Direction. That's not us."

Who said it? ....

5. "A lot of bands have to change what they sound like, but we are exactly the band that we want to be: a pop band, definitely, but we've got a rock and punk edge."

Who said it? ....

6. "We've got like nearly 100 songs written (for the album) because we've been writing for over a year now."

Who said it? ....

7. "We're not trying to be anything that we're not. We're not the new anything. We're the first 5 Seconds Of Summer."

Who said it? ....

8. "(The music is) going to be really guitar driven, very high energy."

Who said it? ....

9. "We just want to be the biggest and the best band that we can be really. See how far we can take it."

Who said it? ....

10. "We like our shows to be a big party vibe, y'know? We want it to be an amazing experience."

Who said it? ....

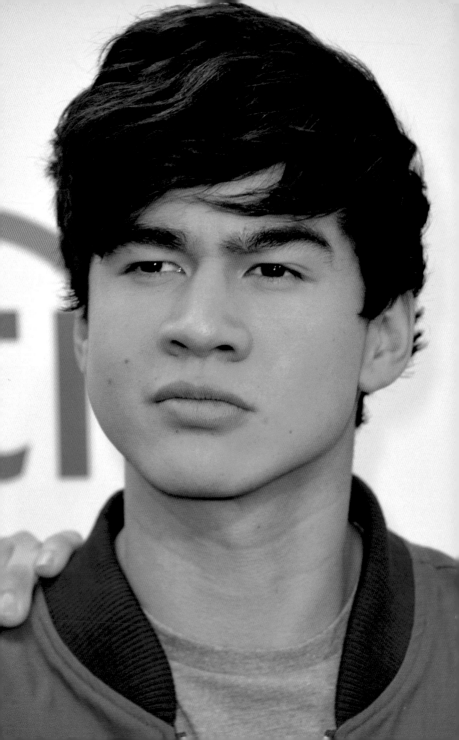

TWEET TIME

CAN YOU GUESS WHICH OF THE TWITTER-TASTIC 5SOS BOYS
SENT THE TWEETS BELOW? WRITE YOUR ANSWER AT THE BOTTOM
OF THE PAGE AND CHECK IT ON **PAGE 93.**

Must be a sign. 3rd pair of ripped jeans in two months

....

My mum gets more texts than me

....

I will let you join the band if you can beat me in FIFA.
Try me

....

Going into deep hibernation due to sickness and efforts
to avoid ghosts

....

You reach your peak ruggedness when you are
modeling for perfume

....

This house smells like teenage boy and cheese toastie

The mystery Tweeter is ....

WOULD YOU RATHER ...

WHAT WOULD HAPPEN IF YOU GOT THE CHANCE TO MEET 5 SECONDS OF SUMMER? HOW WOULD YOU SPEND YOUR TIME TOGETHER? HAVE A LOOK AT THE QUESTIONS BELOW AND PUT A CHECK BY EACH OPTION YOU PREFER. TAKE YOUR TIME, THERE ARE SOME VERY DIFFICULT CHOICES TO MAKE.

Would you rather ...

Let Ashton teach you how to play drums? ☐ ☐ Have a signed pair of Ashton's drumsticks?

Write a song with the band? ☐ ☐ Have the boys write a song about you?

Go shopping with Michael? ☐ ☐ Have Michael design you a special T-shirt?

Let Calum make you your favorite meal? ☐ ☐ Cook a special meal for Calum?

Take Luke to a party to meet your friends? ☐ ☐ Go to Luke's birthday party as a VIP guest?

Interview 5SOS for your school magazine? ☐ ☐ Have the boys say hello to you during a radio interview?

Sing on stage with the band? ☐ ☐ Hang out backstage with 5SOS after the show?

Have Ashton retweet a message from you? ☐ ☐ Have Ashton "like" one of your posts on Facebook?

Have 5SOS perform at your school? ☐ ☐ Go to Australia to watch the boys play a hometown concert?

Decide which color Michael dyes his hair? ☐ ☐ Have Michael choose your next hairstyle?

Have Calum dedicate a song to you at a concert? ☐ ☐ Have Calum sign your favorite shirt?

Decide the title of the next 5SOS album? ☐ ☐ Have your name as the title of a 5SOS song?

Design stage outfits for the band? ☐ ☐ Take a selfie with the boys?

Let Luke sing you his favorite song? ☐ ☐ Sing your favorite 5SOS song to Luke?

★ SO DEEP: MICHAEL VS CALUM ★

EACH OF THE 5 SECONDS OF SUMMER BOYS LOVES TO LET YOU KNOW WHAT'S ON HIS MIND BY SENDING YOU VERY SPECIAL MESSAGES ON TWITTER. CAN YOU TELL IF IT WAS MICHAEL OR CALUM WHO WROTE THE FOLLOWING WORDS OF WISDOM? THE ANSWERS ARE ON **PAGE 93**.

It's the 21st century, why do we still have shoe laces?

☐ Michael   ☐ Calum

Do you ever wish you could forget your favorite movie? just so you could watch it again for the first time

☐ Michael   ☐ Calum

Planning on living forever

☐ Michael   ☐ Calum

I bit my tongue and it hurts to speak so now I speak weird

☐ Michael   ☐ Calum

🐦 Just live right now, and be yourself, it doesn't matter if it's good enough for someone else

☐ Michael ☐ Calum

🐦 i've now learned it's not acceptable to wear white socks on stage

☐ Michael ☐ Calum

🐦 My life is filled of learning from mistakes .. Starting to get ta me a bit!

☐ Michael ☐ Calum

🐦 Something's gotta go wrong cause I'm feelin way too damn good

☐ Michael ☐ Calum

🐦 I wish some people could just listen to themselves argue from an outside perspective and realize how stupid they sound...ridiculous.

☐ Michael ☐ Calum

🐦 Are we only damaging the little we have left?

☐ Michael ☐ Calum

♪TWEET TIME♪

THE 5SOS BOYS HAVE MILLIONS OF FOLLOWERS BETWEEN THEM.
CAN YOU GUESS WHO SENT ALL THE TWEETS BELOW? FIND THE
ANSWER ON **PAGE 94** IF YOU CAN'T FIGURE IT OUT.

🐦 Why is it called having a crush on someone?? strange
choice of words

··

🐦 No TV, check. no wifi, check. no signal, check.
only enough hot water for one shower, check. not near
civilization, check. #5soshouse LOL.

··

🐦 I like to think I speak fluent internet

··

🐦 I lasted 20 minutes outside before I spilt drink on my
white shirt. #itsonpurpose #promise #punk

··

🐦 People who play those dance games in the middle of
shopping malls are very brave

··

🐦 Don't tell anyone but I'm wearing the same jumper today
as I did yesterday and I don't think anyone has noticed

The mystery Tweeter is ·· .

FIRST TIME FOR EVERYTHING

IT'S BEEN A ROLLER-COASTER RIDE FOR THE 5SOS BOYS. THEY'VE FOUND INTERNATIONAL SUCCESS SO QUICKLY THAT THEY'VE HAD LOTS OF FIRST-TIME EXPERIENCES IN A VERY SHORT TIME. ANSWER THE QUESTIONS BELOW TO SEE IF YOU REMEMBER THEIR FIRST TIME FOR EVERYTHING. CHECK THE ANSWERS ON **PAGE 94**.

1. 5SOS's first Australian EP was called *Unplugged*. Which four of these songs appeared on that release? Put a check in the box next to the correct titles.

☐ "Gotta Get Out"   ☐ "Beside You"   ☐ "Jasey Rae"

☐ "Too Late"   ☐ "I Miss You"   ☐ "Bad Dreams"

☐ "Out Of My Limit"   ☐ "Over And Over"

2. Two of the boys had never been to a concert until they played their own with 5SOS. Do you know which pair?
   a. Calum and Luke
   b. Ashton and Michael
   c. Luke and Ashton
   d. Michael and Calum

3. Luke's first trip outside Australia and New Zealand was with the band. What was it for?

   a. A shopping trip to New York

   b. Meeting One Direction in Paris

   c. Song writing trip to London

   d. A birthday trip to Las Vegas

4. Which member of 5 Seconds Of Summer was born first?

   a. Luke

   b. Calum

   c. Michael

   d. Ashton

5. What is the first track on the boys' album?

   a. "Don't Stop"

   b. "She Looks So Perfect"

   c. "Good Girls"

   d. "Everything I Didn't Say"

6. One of the first YouTube videos the boys posted was a cover of Chris Brown and Justin Bieber's "Next To You." Can you name their first solo hit singles?

Chris Brown:	Justin Bieber:
a. "No Air"	a. "Baby"
b. "Beautiful People"	b. "One Time"
c. "Run It!"	c. "Eenie Meenie"
d. "Yo (Excuse Me Miss)"	d. "Boyfriend"

7. 5SOS's first tour was supporting which American band on the Australian leg of their *Whatever World Tour*?

a. Nickelback

b. The Fray

c. Hot Chelle Rae

d. One Republic

8. The first time 5 Seconds Of Summer played live on U.S. TV was at the 2014 Billboard Awards. Which four of the following artists also played that night?

☐ Kanye West   ☐ Lorde

☐ Jennifer Lopez   ☐ Justin Timberlake

☐ Jason Derulo   ☐ Katy Perry

☐ Foo Fighters   ☐ Beyoncé

9. *The Twenty Twelve Tour* was the boys' first mini headline tour. Which Australian city did they visit first?

a. Sydney

b. Brisbane

c. Adelaide

d. Melbourne

10. The boys' first No.1 single outside Australia was "She Looks So Perfect." What is the first word in the song?

a. Simmer

b. Ho

c. Hey

d. Let's

COVER UP

YOU MIGHT HAVE SEEN 5SOS FOR THE FIRST TIME SINGING ANOTHER ARTIST'S SONG ON YOUTUBE, AND THE BOYS STILL LOVE TO CREATE THEIR OWN VERSIONS OF SONGS BY THEIR FAVOURITE ARTISTS. SEE HOW MUCH YOU KNOW ABOUT THE ARTISTS AND MUSIC THAT INSPIRE 5SOS. CHECK YOUR ANSWERS ON **PAGE 94.**

1. 5SOS have covered "Lego House" and "Give Me Love," two songs by English singer/songwriter Ed Sheeran. Can you name the One Direction album on which Ed co-wrote two songs?

....

2. Blink 182 is one of the 5SOS boys' favorite bands. But can you name Blink 182's biggest hit song, which reached No.2 in the Official U.K. Chart and No.6 on Billboard's Hot 100 in America in January 2000?

....

3. "We Are Young," by the band Fun, was one of the biggest hits of 2012 and the 5SOS boys recorded a very special acoustic version for Australian radio station Nova FM. Can you name Fun's lead singer, who also sang with Pink on her hit song, "Just Give Me a Reason"?

....

4. "Rolling in the Deep" was covered by Luke and Calum in a video uploaded to YouTube in August 2011. Can you name the Adele album that features the original version of the song?

....

5. One of the band's best covers contains the lines, "I've got two tickets to Iron Maiden, baby, come with me Friday, don't say maybe." Can you name the original artist and song?

....

6. 5SOS's most famous cover video was a version of "Next To You" by Chris Brown and Justin Bieber. Which Chris Brown album featured the original version of the song?

....

7. The boys uploaded a version of "Year 3000" to YouTube in September 2012. Can you name the band that originally recorded the song in 2002 and also had hits with "Crashed the Wedding," "What I Go To School For" and "Air Hostess"?

....

8. Alex Gaskarth, Jack Barakat, Rian Dawson and Zack Merrick are all members of one of 5 Seconds Of Summer's favorite groups. In early 2012 the boys recorded themselves singing their song, "Jasey Rae." Can you name the band?

....

BANDMATE BANTER

LUKE, MIKE, CALUM, AND ASHTON SPEND A LOT OF TIME HANGING OUT TOGETHER AND TWEETING ABOUT EACH OTHER. CAN YOU GUESS WHO EACH TWEET BELOW IS ABOUT? THE ANSWERS ARE ON **PAGE 94**.

I smell so bad and _____ smells like flowers ....

Calum was Tweeting about ....

_____ is the only guy to carry a plastic sword around at a party and somehow make it cool ...

Ash was Tweeting about ....

I had a dream last night that I had to find _____ in a jungle and when I found him he turned out like the kid from jungle book.. #monkeyman

Michael was Tweeting about ....

🐦 _____ is the only person ever to not like friends.

Calum was Tweeting about ....

🐦 _____ left, but the smell of hairspray remains

Luke was Tweeting about ....

🐦 Got woken up by a wild _____ playing guitar at the end of my bed ...

Calum was Tweeting about ....

🐦 _____'s getting craving, my theory is, he is pregnant

Ashton was Tweeting about ....

🐦 Why does everybody think _____'s 3 feet taller than us... :(

Calum was Tweeting about ....

5SOS FOREVER

LOST FOR WORDS

CAN YOU FIND ALL THE 5SOS-RELATED WORDS OR PHRASES IN THE WORDSEARCH ON THE OPPOSITE PAGE? THEY COULD BE FORWARD, BACKWARD, UP, DOWN, ACROSS, OR DIAGONAL. CHECK TO SEE HOW MANY YOU GOT—THE ANSWERS ARE ON **PAGE 95**.

SHE LOOKS SO PERFECT	PARAMORE
X FACTOR	NORWEST COLLEGE
CAPITOL	HI OR HEY RECORDS
WILL SMITH	NANDOS
GOTTA GET OUT	RICHMOND HIGH
TAKE ME HOME	ALEX GASKARTH

B	R	A	X	G	D	P	F	P	A	H	L	C	K	G	M	B	I	A	W
E	G	E	L	L	O	C	T	S	E	W	R	O	N	O	U	S	D	Y	E
R	I	C	H	M	O	N	D	H	I	G	H	E	G	T	S	G	W	A	Z
E	A	N	J	D	M	Y	W	E	F	I	Q	L	O	T	M	B	W	N	T
A	J	T	L	K	A	B	H	L	A	E	A	V	H	A	U	C	I	A	P
L	P	A	R	S	G	Z	N	O	J	Q	T	K	J	G	S	Y	F	N	C
E	N	N	F	K	P	H	I	O	R	H	E	Y	R	E	C	O	R	D	S
X	S	C	P	C	U	W	E	K	C	X	L	P	H	T	W	S	L	O	T
G	K	E	Y	A	M	B	H	S	M	F	T	H	K	O	O	D	Y	S	M
A	T	G	L	P	D	X	K	S	M	A	I	C	G	U	S	B	K	U	J
S	W	Y	I	I	L	A	P	O	F	C	N	X	V	T	T	E	A	W	T
K	O	I	Q	T	F	Z	H	P	N	T	J	A	G	W	E	H	K	F	A
A	S	J	L	O	S	G	E	E	A	O	I	K	C	A	I	O	D	I	L
R	E	D	P	L	M	A	O	R	U	R	M	G	H	A	R	D	N	P	E
T	Q	A	G	W	S	T	C	F	F	W	A	Y	K	E	X	B	W	A	Q
H	F	X	J	K	F	M	V	E	M	H	W	M	U	S	I	E	J	T	U
J	V	B	O	W	D	S	I	C	Z	B	K	N	O	C	L	D	D	F	A
F	O	D	E	M	A	K	P	T	Y	T	G	E	P	R	P	O	B	U	P
A	T	G	T	A	K	E	M	E	H	O	M	E	C	D	E	Z	T	I	Y
V	E	X	W	N	L	K	H	C	Y	A	S	E	W	G	E	E	S	U	A

FAVORITE THINGS

CAN YOU TELL WHICH LIST OF FAVORITE THINGS BELONGS TO EACH OF THE BOYS IN THE BAND? WRITE YOUR ANSWER UNDER EACH LIST AND CHECK IF YOU'VE GOT IT RIGHT ON **PAGE 95.**

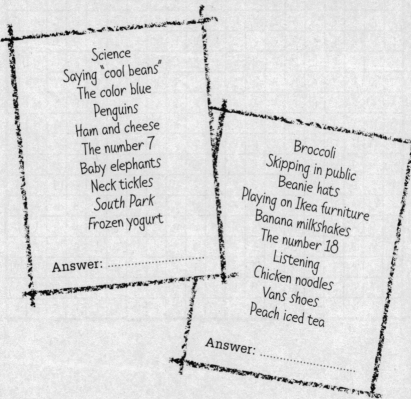

Science
Saying "cool beans"
The color blue
Penguins
Ham and cheese
The number 7
Baby elephants
Neck tickles
South Park
Frozen yogurt

Answer: ....

Broccoli
Skipping in public
Beanie hats
Playing on Ikea furniture
Banana milkshakes
The number 18
Listening
Chicken noodles
Vans shoes
Peach iced tea

Answer: ....

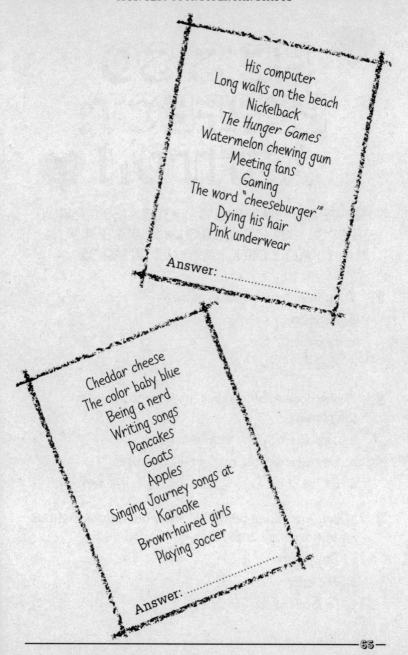

His computer
Long walks on the beach
Nickelback
The Hunger Games
Watermelon chewing gum
Meeting fans
Gaming
The word "cheeseburger'"
Dying his hair
Pink underwear

Answer: ....

Cheddar cheese
The color baby blue
Being a nerd
Writing songs
Pancakes
Goats
Apples
Singing Journey songs at
Karaoke
Brown-haired girls
Playing soccer

Answer: ....

HE'S SO PERFECT: ASHTON

HERE ARE EIGHT BRAIN TEASING QUESTIONS ABOUT ASHTON.
SEE IF YOU KNOW HIM WELL ENOUGH TO ANSWER THEM ALL
CORRECTLY. CHECK HOW YOU DID ON **PAGE 95**.

1. What is Ashton's middle name?
   a. Fletcher
   b. Finlay
   c. Freddie

2. Where does Ashton say is his favorite place on the planet?
   a. Shopping in Sydney with his family
   b. On stage with the rest of the 5SOS boys
   c. On top of the Empire State Building in New York

3. Which Australian television show did Ashton audition for in November 2010?
   a. The X Factor
   b. The Voice
   c. So You Think You Can Dance

4. Who did Ashton say makes a "bangin" cup of tea'?
   a. His mom
   b. His cousin
   c. His little brother

5. What is Ashton's superhero alter-ego name in the "Don't Stop" music video?
   a. Ash-Man
   b. The Masher
   c. Smash

6. What is Ashton's favorite television show?
   a. Family Guy
   b. The Simpsons
   c. Futurama

7. Why does Ashton say he hated 5 Seconds Of Summer before he joined the band?
   a. They were all so much better looking than him
   b. They were always messing around and forgetting the words in their YouTube videos
   c. More girls went to their concerts than to his band's gigs

8. What was the name of one of Ashton's other bands before he joined 5SOS?
   a. Swallow the Goldfish
   b. Fire With Fire
   c. Flying Fish

A HELPING ♥ HAND

THE BOYS ARE LOOKING FOR A PERSONAL ASSISTANT FOR THEIR NEXT TOUR. DO YOU HAVE WHAT IT TAKES TO MAKE THE BOYS KEEP TO THEIR VERY BUSY SCHEDULE? ANSWER THE QUESTIONS BELOW AND SEE IF YOU'VE MADE THE GRADE ON **PAGE 72**.

1. The boys need to be up at five in the morning for an important TV interview, but they are refusing to go to bed until they have watched every Will Smith DVD. What do you do?

a. Take all the television equipment out of their rooms

b. Tell them if they go to bed now, you'll set up a Will Smith-themed party for the following evening

c. Sit down with the boys to watch the movie

2. Everyone is waiting in the hotel lobby to be taken to the interview, but the limos haven't showed up. What do you do?

a. Persuade the kind manager of the hotel to drive you all there

b. Flag down a cab outside the hotel

c. Cancel the interview and go back to bed

3. You finally arrive with the boys, but because you're late you have been told they won't be allowed to perform their new single. What do you do?

   a. Be so persuasive that the TV show drops another guest completely and allows the band to perform two songs in their time slot instead

   b. Demand that they cut down the number of questions to let the boys sing a shorter version of their single

   c. Agree to cut the song and have a coffee in the cafeteria while the boys are being interviewed

4. After the interview you are taking the boys to a secret location to film their new video. The only problem is you can't remember where it is. What do you do?

   a. Call the video director to meet you at the TV studio and take you from there

   b. Realize you've thought ahead and left a note in your phone that tells you the shoot location.

   c. Try to film the video yourself with your phone camera

5. You get to the video shoot to find the dancers haven't been given the correct address and are stuck on the other side of the city. What do you do?

   a. Move the whole video shoot to where the dancers are. You can be flexible

   b. Send cars to pick up the dancers and bring them to you

   c. Volunteer to do all the dancing yourself

6. The boys take a break from the shoot for lunch, but the catering van hasn't shown up. What do you do?

   a. Take the boys for a four-course lunch at an expensive restaurant

   b. Get some pizzas delivered to the video set. Speed is of the essence

   c. Let the boys share a sandwich from your packed lunch. They don't need more than a bite each

7. The video is done and it looks amazing. Now the boys need to head over to the concert venue for their sound-check. Unfortunately, the boys want to do some shopping beforehand. What do you do?

   a. Make some calls and get a local shopping mall closed to the public so the boys can shop in private

   b. Arrange for the boys to do a record signing at a local store and they can meet some fans and do their shopping at the same time

   c. Tell the boys they don't have time to go shopping

8. The boys have turned up at the venue and none of their instruments are there. What do you do?

   a. Send someone out to buy all new equipment. You have to get this done

   b. Ask the support band if the 5SOS boys can borrow their instruments

   c. Tell the boys they can't perform

9. The opening band shows up, but they are all feeling very unwell and can't do the show. What do you do?

   a. Call One Direction and tell them to come along to open the show

   b. You tell the boys they don't need an opening act because they are so amazing

   c. Cancel the show

10. Halfway through the show, the venue loses power to the stage area and none of the electric instruments are working. What do you do?

   a. Give everyone a refund

   b. Let the boys carry on with an acoustic set and let their pure talent shine through

   c. Try to fix the electrics yourself; you know you've read a book on this at some point

Now count up your answers and turn the page to see if you're perfect for the role, or could do better ...

SCORE YOURSELF

IF YOU SCORED MOSTLY 'A'S ...

You're the boss. Forget about becoming their PA, the boys want you to be their new manager. You know how to solve every problem and can pull all the strings to make anything happen. With you by their side they will soon be the biggest band in the world ... maybe even the Universe.

IF YOU SCORED MOSTLY 'B'S ...

You're the cool-headed fixer. Cool, calm, and collected, you are exactly what the boys are looking for. You keep a level head when everyone else is in a panic. You work well under pressure and use your quick wits to solve any problem that's thrown at you. If working for the boys doesn't work out, maybe you should go into politics; it looks like you could fix just about everything.

IF YOU SCORED MOSTLY 'C'S ...

You're not so perfect. Oh dear! The boys might be back performing on the streets or flipping burgers if you're left in charge. You don't really seem up for the task and you should probably give up your dream of going on tour with 5 Seconds Of Summer as their PA. But they still need someone to sell T-shirts at the venue ... so you never know.

POP THE QUESTION

IMAGINE YOU ARE WORKING AT THE WORLD'S MOST FAMOUS MUSIC MAGAZINE AND 5 SECONDS OF SUMMER ARE COMING TO GIVE YOU AN EXCLUSIVE INTERVIEW. IT'S UP TO YOU TO THINK UP SOME INTERESTING QUESTIONS THAT WILL GIVE YOU THE ULTIMATE SCOOP.

Ask Calum something about his childhood.

....

....

....

Ask Luke something about being in a band.

....

....

....

Ask Ashton something about his friends.

....

....

....

Ask Michael something about the 5SOS fans.

....

....

....

Ask Calum something about One Direction.

....

....

....

Ask Luke something about becoming famous.

....

....

....

Ask Ashton something about playing the drums.

....

....

....

Ask Michael something about the perfect date.

....

....

....

Ask Calum something about traveling around the world.

....

....

....

Ask Luke something about food.

....

....

....

Ask Ashton something about making music.

....

....

....

Ask Michael something about his family.

....

....

....

Now you've created the ultimate interview; why not get a fellow fan to answer the questions as the boys? See what answers you get!

AMERICAN BOYS

IT HASN'T TAKEN LONG FOR 5SOS TO BECOME WORLDWIDE NAMES. IN JUNE 2013 THE BOYS TOOK THEIR FIRST TRIP TO MEET THEIR AMERICAN FANS AND THEY'VE SINCE GONE BACK FOR MORE. HOW MUCH DO YOU KNOW ABOUT HOW THEY CONQUERED AMERICA? CHECK YOUR ANSWERS ON **PAGE 95**.

1. How many copies did the *She Looks So Perfect* EP sell during its first week on sale in America?
   a. 17,000
   b. 143,000
   c. 204,000

2. Can you name the city where the boys opened their first American headline tour in April 2014?
   a. San Francisco
   b. Dallas
   c. Chicago

3. On which music award show did 5 Seconds Of Summer make their U.S. television debut?
   a. 2014 Grammy Awards
   b. 2014 MTV Music Awards
   c. 2014 Billboard Music Awards

4. Which album kept 5SOS's debut EP, *She Looks So Perfect*, off the U.S. No.1 spot when it was released in March 2014?

a. Katy Perry–Prism

b. Disney's Frozen–Original Soundtrack

c. Pharrell Williams–Girl

5. Can you remember the name the boys gave their first American tour?

a. The Red, White and Blue Tour

b. The Stars, Stripes, and Maple Syrup Tour

c. The Perfect Party Tour

6. Which city hosted 5SOS's last concert when they played alongside One Direction on the American leg of the *Where We Are Tour*?

a. Miami

b. Atlanta

c. Nashville

7. How many minutes did it take for all ten dates on the first 5 Seconds Of Summer U.S. solo tour to sell out?

a. 5 minutes

b. 25 minutes

c. 45 minutes

IN THE HOOD

YOU'RE ON THE TRIP OF A LIFETIME AROUND AUSTRALIA, AND YOUR LAST STOP BEFORE HEADING HOME IS DROPPING IN ON YOUR BEST FRIEND WHO MOVED ALL THE WAY TO SYDNEY LAST SUMMER. OF COURSE YOU'RE EXCITED TO SEE HER AGAIN, BUT YOU ARE NEVER GOING TO BELIEVE WHO LIVES NEXT DOOR ...

It's the day after your arrival in Sydney. You've spent the whole day with your best friend ...., catching up on all the gossip and finding out everything about her new life in Australia. She tells you about this new band she likes, "They're called 5 Seconds Of Summer. Have you heard of them?"

"Heard of them? They are AMAZING!" you say, before adding, "They are the best thing since ...." (One Direction/ The Wanted/ Little Mix)

Your friend then tells you that she actually lives next door to .... (Luke/ Calum/ Ashton/ Michael), and she has become quite friendly with him and his family. "Obviously, he's hardly ever around these days, but we have hung out a few times when he's here. In fact he's invited us to a .... (pool party / BBQ / Will Smith movie marathon) at their place tomorrow."

You can't believe what you're hearing. "Oh, and the rest of the band will be there, too," says your friend. OMG! There's no time to lose, you need to decide what to wear.

After a few hours of frantic shopping you have your outfit, which is a T-shirt with the slogan .... ("You Complete Me"/ "Challenge Accepted"/ "Kiss Me Kiss Me") and your favorite shorts. You pick out your favorite, most comfortable shoes, a pair of .... (strappy sandals/ flip-flops/ sporty sneakers); it's going to be a long day!

As soon as you arrive your friend introduces you to all the boys. Calum says, "Hi," before asking if you'd like .... (a burger/ an autograph/ to see his new tattoo). Of course you say yes! Then you take a selfie with you pointing at it. Ashton asks, "................................... .... ?" (Have you seen much of Sydney's famous landmarks/ Do you have a favorite 5SOS video/ Do you like drummers)

You reply, "... .... " (Yes, but I don't have much free time/ Yes, I like them all/ Yes, I like what I've seen so far).

Of course it doesn't take long before the conversation turns to Will Smith and Michael asks you to name your favorite of his movies.

You say, "... "
(I haven't seen any./ Independence Day./ Who's Will Smith?)

Michael looks shocked and says, "...
.... " (That's okay, I forgive you./ I think I need to show
you my favorite./ Err ... what?)

Next, Luke pulls you aside and asks if you want to ....
....
(listen to a brand new song the boys have just recorded/ cool off
and take a dip in the pool/ eat a pizza). You say, "......................
...." (Of course, but
only if my friend can join us/ Thanks, but I think it's getting late/
I'd love to but I'm stuffed) All the boys laugh and promise to
take you and your friend out the next day to see the sights.

You all swap numbers and say goodnight to the boys and
each one gives you .... (a kiss goodnight/
a signed photograph/ a cupcake).

You're very excited about your day out with the boys
tomorrow and head off to bed to make sure you get plenty
of sleep. You dream about .... (Luke/
Calum/ Michael/ Ashton) taking you for a ....
.... (surfing lesson/ candlelit dinner/
private tour of their recording studio).

When you wake up it's a beautiful sunny day and you are

all ready to go when there is a knock at the door. The boys have sent a private car to pick you both up. The driver has some bad news. Three of the boys have had to cancel

because .... ,
(they have been called into the recording studio/ they slept through their alarms/ they can't decide what to wear) so only one of the boys will be able to join you on your day out.

The good news is that it's your favorite, ...
 (Luke/ Ashton/ Michael/ Calum), who will be joining you. And in the end it turns out to be the perfect day. You visit Sydney Harbour and have your picture taken in front of

.... (a human statue/ the Opera House/ one of the boys' first concert venues). Next, you hit the

beach and spend hours ....
(sunbathing/ kicking a football around/ splashing in the surf).

All too soon it's time to go home and you and your friend say goodbye to your very special 5SOS date. In the car on the way home you say, "..

....................." (This was the best day ever/ I want to remember this forever/ This day couldn't be more perfect) Suddenly a text

arrives on your phone; it's from .... (Ashton/ Luke/ Michael/ Calum) and it says, "...

...." (I'll visit you when I'm next in your hometown/ I've already written a song about meeting you/ It was nice to meet you and I'll never forget you) You can't believe it. This is the perfect end to the best holiday ever!

SHAME ON
★ YOU ★

THE 5SOS BOYS HAVE SOME EMBARRASSING SECRETS AND STORIES THEY'D RATHER YOU DIDN'T KNOW. CAN YOU TELL WHICH OF THESE CRINGE MOMENTS ARE TRUE OR FALSE? MARK THE BOX BESIDE EACH STATEMENT. FIND THE ANSWERS ON **PAGE 96**.

1. When the boys asked Ashton to join the band they promised there would be "200 screaming fans" at their first concert, but there were fewer than 15 people.

☐ True   ☐ False

2. Luke almost turned down joining One Direction on their *Take Me Home Tour* because he was worried he would get homesick.

☐ True   ☐ False

3. The band had to street perform for money after one gig because they had run out of cash and needed to get home.

☐ True   ☐ False

4. Ashton had to play the part of Juliet in a school production of *Romeo and Juliet*.

☐ True   ☐ False

5. Calum once had to fix his pants with duct tape after they split while he was on stage.

☐ True   ☐ False

6. Ashton is afraid of ducks.

☐ True   ☐ False

7. Luke cries every time he watches the film *Titanic*.

☐ True   ☐ False

8. Luke's secret passion is moisturizing.

☐ True   ☐ False

9. Ashton didn't learn how to tie his shoe laces until he had joined the band.

☐ True   ☐ False

10. Calum refuses to travel with the band. He prefers to read romantic fan fiction in peace, alone.

☐ True   ☐ False

11. The boys got properly thrashed during a friendly football match with One Direction. Embarrassing!

☐ True   ☐ False

12. The boys celebrated Calum's 18th birthday at a club, but had to show ID at the door to prove who they were.

☐ True   ☐ False

MOVIE NIGHT

CALUM, ASHTON, MICHAEL AND LUKE SPEND LOTS OF TIME ON TOUR WATCHING FILMS – AND SOMETIMES THEY EVEN MANAGE TO WATCH ONE THAT DOESN'T FEATURE WILL SMITH! CAN YOU GUESS WHICH MOVIES THE BOYS ARE TALKING ABOUT BELOW? ANSWERS ARE ON **PAGE 96**.

1. Ashton: "This could be one of the best movies I've seen, feelings of loneliness, love, depression, and happiness, loved it!"
   a. Her
   b. Gravity
   c. Captain Phillips

2. Calum says that after watching this film, Leonardo Di Caprio became his favorite actor—behind Will Smith, of course.
   a. Titanic
   b. The Great Gatsby
   c. The Wolf of Wall Street

3. Michael said about this film: "I've only just got on the … hype train … I'm like two months late."
   a. Despicable Me 2
   b. The Lego Movie
   c. Frozen

4. Luke watched this film on Valentine's Day, and said, "Now I know how it feels to be a girl."

   a. Dirty Dancing

   b. Bridget Jones' Diary

   c. Mamma Mia

5. You know Ashton loves Will Smith, but which film made him Tweet "Will Smith is my all time favourite actor, of all time... Ever"?

   a. After Earth

   b. I Am Legend

   c. 7 Pounds

6. This film prompted Calum to Tweet "I'm scared :(."

   a. Carrie

   b. The Conjuring

   c. The Hunger Games: Catching Fire

7. Michael said that this film was "the funniest yet weirdest thing" he'd ever seen. What is it?

   a. Anchorman 2

   b. We're the Millers

   c. The Heat

8. Luke described this film as "literally amazing."

   a. The Lego Movie

   b. Thor: The Dark World

   c. Divergent

CRUSH ON YOU

EVERY MEMBER OF 5 SECONDS OF SUMMER HAS MADE IT VERY CLEAR WHO THEIR CELEBRITY CRUSHES ARE—AND THERE ARE QUITE A FEW OF THEM! PUT A CHECK IN THE BOX NEXT TO THE NAMES OF THE BOYS' TRUE CRUSHES. ANSWERS ON **PAGE 96**.

ASHTON

1. Pink

2. Jade Thirlwall from Little Mix

3. Jessie J

4. Rita Ora

5. Hayley Williams from Paramore

6. Rihanna

CALUM

1. Katy Perry

2. Delta Goodrem

3. Alicia Keys

4. Kylie Minogue

5. Taylor Swift

6. Jessica Alba

LUKE

☐ **1.** Mila Kunis

☐ **2.** Vanessa Hudgens

☐ **3.** Shailene Woodley

☐ **4.** Jennifer Lawrence

☐ **5.** Emma Stone

☐ **6.** Demi Lovato

MICHAEL

☐ **1.** Chloe Moretz

☐ **2.** Lady GaGa

☐ **3.** Camila Cabello from 5th Harmony

☐ **4.** Ellie Goulding

☐ **5.** Ariana Grande

☐ **6.** Emilly Bett Rickards

BEST BOY

MICHAEL, ASHTON, LUKE, AND CALUM ARE ALL TOTALLY AMAZING, BUT NOW YOU CAN FIND OUT WHICH ONE OF THE BOYS REALLY IS THE BEST. JUST GIVE EACH OF THE BOYS MARKS OUT OF TEN IN THE FOLLOWING CATEGORIES, ADD UP ALL THEIR SCORES AND THE GRAND TOTALS WILL REVEAL WHO IS "BEST BOY."

1. COOL HAIR

Ashton .... out of 10

Calum .... out of 10

Michael .... out of 10

Luke .... out of 10

2. STYLISH CLOTHES

Ashton .... out of 10

Calum .... out of 10

Michael .... out of 10

Luke .... out of 10

3. MUSICAL TALENT

Ashton .... out of 10

Calum .... out of 10

Michael .... out of 10

Luke .... out of 10

4. INTERVIEW BANTER

Ashton .... out of 10

Calum .... out of 10

Michael .... out of 10

Luke .... out of 10

5. GOOD LOOKS

Ashton .... out of 10

Calum .... out of 10

Michael .... out of 10

Luke .... out of 10

7. STAGE PERFORMANCE

Ashton .... out of 10

Calum .... out of 10

Michael .... out of 10

Luke .... out of 10

6. BEST TWEETS

Ashton .... out of 10

Calum .... out of 10

Michael .... out of 10

Luke .... out of 10

8. BEST BOYFRIEND

Ashton .... out of 10

Calum .... out of 10

Michael .... out of 10

Luke .... out of 10

FILL IN THE BOYS' SCORES HERE:

Ashton ....+.......+.......+.......+.......+.......+.......+........ = ... out of 80

Calum ....+.......+.......+.......+.......+.......+.......+........ = ... out of 80

Michael ....+.......+.......+.......+.......+.......+.......+........ = ... out of 80

Luke ....+.......+.......+.......+.......+.......+.......+........ = ... out of 80

THE 5SOS "BEST BOY" IS: ....

ALL THE ANSWERS

Perfect Ten
Pages 6–8

1. c	4. c	7. b	10. a
2. a	5. b	8. c	
3. a	6. a	9. b	

He's So Perfect: Michael
Pages 9–10

1. a	4. a	7. b
2. a	5. c	8. a
3. b	6. a	

Food For Thought
Page 11
In order of appearance, the Tweets were posted by:
Luke, Michael, Ashton, Luke, Calum, Ashton

The Story Of Us
Pages 12–15
In order of appearance, the answers are: college, 2011, YouTube, drummer, December, *Unplugged*, Louis Tomlinson, Kaiser Chiefs, *Take Me Home*, London, Capitol, 100, Billboard, Best International Newcomer, *5 Seconds Of Summer*, Dublin, Scott Mills, the World Cup

So Deep: Luke Vs Ashton
Pages 16–17

1.	Luke	4.	Ashton	7.	Luke	10.	Ashton
2.	Luke	5.	Luke	8.	Ashton		
3.	Ashton	6.	Luke	9.	Ashton		

He's So Perfect: Luke
Pages 18–19

1.	a	4.	c	7.	b
2.	b	5.	a	8.	b
3.	b	6.	a		

Crack That Crossword
Pages 20–21

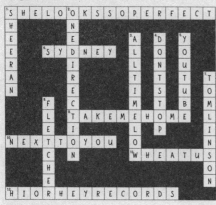

Who Said It?
Pages 22–23

1.	Ashton	4.	Ashton	7.	Michael
2.	Ashton	5.	Michael	8.	Michael
3.	Calum	6.	Ashton	9.	Michael

Tweet Time
Page 24
The mystery Tweeter is Ashton

1D Buddies
Page 25

1. Louis Tomlinson
2. The *Where We Are Tour*
3. *One Thing*
4. Sunshine, Florida
5. Michael Clifford

Fans For Everything
Pages 26–27

1. Ashton
2. Luke
3. Ashton
4. Calum
5. Calum
6. Michael
7. Luke
8. Michael

Secret Gig
Pages 28–30

1. The gig venue is MGM Grand Garden Arena, Las Vegas
2. The gig will take place on January 18 at 7PM
3. The special guest is Katy Perry
4. Use entrance number 12, row F, seat number 20
5. The secret combination is 96-3-2-16

Tweet Time
Page 31
The mystery Tweeter is Luke

He's So Perfect: Calum
Pages 32–33

1. c	4. a	7. c
2. b	5. b	8. a
3. b	6. a	

Song Scramble
Pages 45–46

1. "She Looks So Perfect"	5. "Out Of My Limit"
2. "Heartbreak Girl"	6. "English Love Affair"
3. "Next To You"	7. "Good Girls"
4. "Don't Stop"	8. "Beside You"

Who We Are
Pages 47–48

1. Ashton	4. Ashton	7. Luke	10. Luke
2. Michael	5. Luke	8. Luke	
3. Luke	6. Ashton	9. Ashton	

Tweet Time
Page 49
The mystery Tweeter is Calum

So Deep: Michael Vs Calum
Pages 52–53

1. Michael	4. Calum	7. Calum	10. Michael
2. Michael	5. Calum	8. Calum	
3. Calum	6. Michael	9. Michael	

Tweet Time
Page 54
The mystery Tweeter is Michael

First Time For Everything
Pages 55–57

1. "Gotta Get Out," "I Miss You," "Too Late" and "Jasey Rae"
2. d
3. c
4. d
5. b
6. Chris Brown "Run It" and Justin Bieber "One Time"
7. c
8. Jennifer Lopez, Jason Derulo, Lorde, and Katy Perry
9. c
10. c

Cover Up
Pages 58–59

1. *Take Me Home*
2. "All The Small Things"
3. Nate Ruess
4. '21'
5. Wheatus—"Teenage Dirtbag"
6. *F.A.M.E.*
7. Busted
8. All Time Low

Bandmate Banter
Pages 60–61

1. Luke
2. Michael
3. Calum
4. Luke
5. Michael
6. Ashton
7. Luke
8. Luke

Lost For Words
Pages 62–63

B	R	A	X	G	D	P	F	P	A	H	L	C	K	S	M	B	I	A	W
E	G	E	L	L	O	C	T	J	E	W	R	O	N	O	U	S	D	Y	E
R	I	C	H	M	O	N	D	J	I	G	H	E	G	T	S	G	W	A	Z
E	A	N	J	D	M	Y	W	F	I	Q	L	O	T	M	B	W	N	T
A	J	T	L	K	A	B	H	A	E	A	V	H	A	U	C	I	A	P
I	P	A	R	S	G	Z	N	O	J	Q	T	K	J	G	S	Y	F	N	C
L	N	N	F	K	P	H	I	O	R	H	E	Y	R	E	C	O	R	D	S
A	S	C	P	G	U	W	E	K	C	X	L	P	H	T	W	S	L	O	T
G	K	E	Y	A	M	B	H	S	M	E	T	H	K	O	O	D	Y	S	M
A	T	G	L	P	D	X	K	S	M	A	I	C	G	U	S	B	K	U	J
S	W	Y	I	L	A	P	O	F	C	N	X	V	T	T	E	A	W	T
K	O	N	Q	F	Z	H	N	T	J	A	G	W	E	H	K	F	A
A	S	J	O	S	G	E	O	I	K	C	A	I	O	D	I	L
R	E	D	P	M	A	O	U	M	G	H	A	R	D	N	P	E
T	Q	A	G	W	T	C	F	W	Y	K	E	X	B	W	A	Q
U	F	X	J	K	F	V	M	H	W	U	S	I	E	J	T	U
F	O	D	E	M	A	K	P	Y	T	G	E	P	P	O	B	U	P
A	T	G	T	A	K	E	M	E	H	O	M	E	C	D	S	Z	T	I	Y
V	E	X	W	N	L	K	H	C	Y	A	S	E	W	G	E	E	S	U	A

Favorite Things
Pages 64–65
In the order the lists appear, they belong to:
Luke, Michael, Ashton, Calum

He's So Perfect: Ashton
Pages 66–67

1.	a	4.	c	7.	a
2.	b	5.	a	8.	a
3.	b	6.	b		

American Boys
Pages 76–77

1.	b	4.	b	7.	a
2.	a	5.	b		
3.	c	6.	a		

Shame On You
Pages 82–83

1.	True	4.	False	7.	False	10.	False
2.	False	5.	True	8.	True	11.	True
3.	True	6.	True	9.	False	12.	True

Movie Night
Pages 84–85

1.	a	4.	b	7.	a
2.	c	5.	c	8.	a
3.	c	6.	b		

Crush On You
Pages 86–87

Ashton's crushes are Pink, Jade Thirlwall from Little Mix, and Hayley Williams from Paramore

Calum's crushes are Katy Perry, Delta Goodrem, Alicia Keys, and Jessica Alba

Luke's crushes are Mila Kunis and Jennifer Lawrence

Michael's crushes are Chloe Moretz, Camila Cabello from 5th Harmony, Ariana Grande, and Emily Bett Rickards